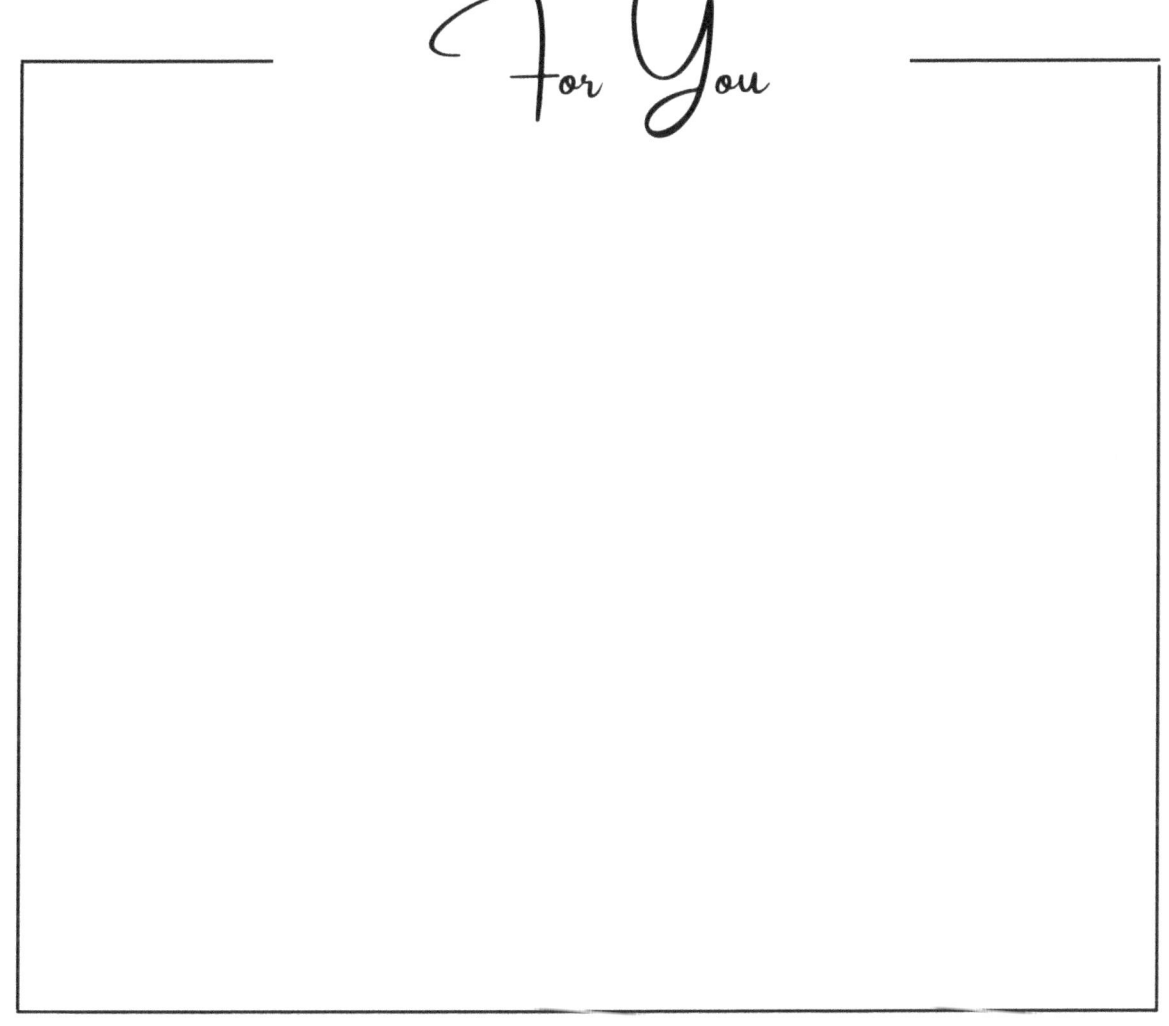

FOR ELFRIEDE

COOKIES AND LOVE
Published by LHC Publishing 2022

Text Copyright © 2022 Y. Eevi Jones
Illustrations Copyright © 2022 Y. Eevi Jones
Cover Design by Y. Eevi Jones
Cover Art by Anna Ismagilova

Printed in the USA.

All the characters in this book are fictitious, and any resemblance to actual persons living or dead is purely coincidental.

All rights reserved. No part of this publication may be reproduced, distributed, or transmitted in any form or by any means, or stored in a database or retrieval system, without the prior written permission of the copyright holder.

All inquiries should be directed to
www.LHCpublishing.com

ISBN-13: 978-1-952517-19-8 Paperback
ISBN-13: 978-1-952517-18-1 Hardcover

Life's Biggest Moments
COOKIES & LOVE

For the Best Grandparents in the World

WRITTEN BY
EEVI JONES

For You

Whether Nana, Opa, Mima, Gramps,
Abuela, Granny, Pops;
these words – they stand for love.
A love that never stops.

Golden in your heart.
Silver in your hair.
A treasure through and through,
you're a gem beyond compare.

Giver of best hugs,
you shape moments that will last;
making worlds a little sweeter,
by telling stories 'bout the past.

You teach me 'bout the world long gone,
how things - they used to be.
Like waiting for the phone to ring,
and nightly sign-offs on TV.

Keeper of traditions,
you share cherished memories,
where hardships were not feared
but seen as opportunities.

Holding wisdom of a lifetime,
from which I get to draw each day,
you nourish and preserve my roots,
so my roots don't fade away.

The biggest of hearts, warmest of hugs,
patience so deep and wide.
Sprinkled with advice and hope,
you love, support, and guide.

Priceless, loved, and cherished
are your letters, calls, and notes.
Bridging times apart,
you send cookies made of oats.

Playing hide and seek,
swimming in the pool.
Ice cream cones and holding hands
at pick-up after school.

Bandaids at the ready,
you care for boo-boos and scraped knees.
Kissing tears away,
blowing noses when they sneeze.

Always making time,
for pretend-play, games, and art.
In person, on the phone,
or via Zoom when far apart.

Laughing at my jokes you've heard
a thousand times before,
you're crawling as my pony
on all fours across the floor.

Giving mom and dad a break,
you babysit and share
your time and love so selflessly,
which, I'm aware, is rare.

My childhood without your love,
it wouldn't be the same.
Like trees without their roots.
Like storms without the rain.

Your presence shows me daily
that you're always there for me.
Whether happy, nervous, sad;
whether silly as can be.

All the wisdom and words you're providing
I will never, ever forget.
And once fully grown, living a life of my own,
they will be lived by and cherished instead.

You're there for me, watch out for me.
You unfailingly go beyond and above.
Forevermore, I love you
for your unending hugs, cookies, and love.

ABOUT THE AUTHOR

Writing under a number of pen names, Eevi Jones is a USA Today & WSJ bestselling and award-winning author and ghostwriter of children's books.

Born in former East Germany to a German mother and a Vietnamese father, Eevi loves to infuse her books with racial diversity. She is the founder of Children's Book University where dreams really do come true. **"Life's Biggest Moments" is Eevi's first series for adults.**

Eevi has been featured in media outlets such as Forbes, Scary Mommy, Business Insider, Huffington Post, and Exceptional Parent Magazine, and lives near D.C. with her husband and two boys.

She can be found online at www.BravingTheWorldBooks.com.

A WORD BY THE AUTHOR

Grandparents are precious, so I hope that with the creation of this book, you have discovered yet another wonderful way through which you can show and share your appreciation and love for them. How lucky we are to have such beautiful, never-ending, unconditional love and support in our lives.

If this book touched you in any way, it would mean the world to me if you would take a short moment to leave a heartfelt review. Thank you.

OTHER WORKS BY THIS AUTHOR

 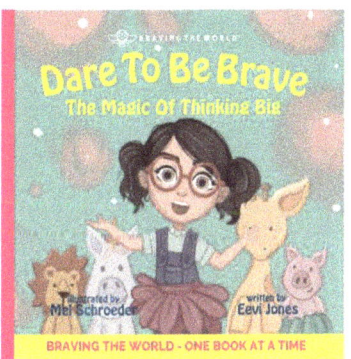 

... AND MANY MORE

www.ingramcontent.com/pod-product-compliance
Lightning Source LLC
Chambersburg PA
CBHW040001290426
43673CB00077B/299